Profit Sharing Formula App

-

Jack's Curated Business Idea

-

Jack Lookman

Profit Sharing Formula App

Jack's Curated Business Idea

Copyright © 2023 Jack Lookman Limited

All rights reserved.
No portion of this book may be reproduced in whole or in part, in any form or by any means, electronic or mechanical including photocopying, recording, or by any information storage and retrieval system, without the consent and written permission from the author.

A. ACKNOWLEDGEMENT

The foundational sacrifices of my parents are much appreciated.

I was fortified with spiritual and academic knowledge and practices; as well as great life skills.

Contributions of John Tosin Adekunle are appreciated.

Taiwo and Owolabi you are also appreciated.

Pastor Dumisani, thank you.

Roland Owolabi, you are appreciated.

Also Seyi Sikirat, thank you.

Chinedu China, I appreciate you.

My beautiful Tolu Mayowa Tobi you are very much appreciated.

To all those who've added value to me, I say, thank you.

jacksempowerment.com. jacklookman.co.uk.
jaaloo.com

B. DEDICATION

This piece of work is dedicated to all my family members.

My Late Dad

My Mum

My Siblings

My Children

May Allah grant us the best of this world and the hereafter and protect us from the torment of hell fire, the grave, and all torments. Ameen.

jacksempowerment.com. jacklookman.co.uk.
jaaloo.com

Profit Sharing Formula App
2

A. ACKNOWLEDGEMENT
3

B. DEDICATION
4

1. Introduction
10

2. What's the idea?
10

3. Inspiration for the idea
11

4. Some requirements for creating the app
11

5. What are the benefits of the app?
12

6. Here are some possible threats to creating a Profit Sharing Formula App.
13

7. Who needs the Profit Sharing Formula App?
14

8. Opportunities for collaboration
14

9. How does the Profit Sharing Formula App work?
14

10. Jack Lookman, have you done a video previously?
16

11. What's the monetisation plan?
16

12. What's the marketing plan?
17

13. Could I make passive income?
17

14. Is it for businesses or projects?
18

15. What data needs to be inputted?
18

16. What's the output data?
19

17. Is this effective stakeholder management?
19

18. Who are the target audience?
19

19. Could collaborations be done virtually?
20

20. About Jack Lookman
20

21. What are the price plans for the Profit Sharing Formula App?
21

22. How could the app be accessed?
21

23. Could the app be synchronized?
21

24. On what gadgets could the app be used?
22

25. Is the app suitable for small or big businesses?
22

26. How could I build the app?
22

27. Disclaimer
22

28. Some legalities to consider
23

29. Possible opportunities from the Profit Sharing Formula App
23

30. What problem is being solved?
24

31. Who will fund the project?
24

32. How could risks be managed?
24

32.1. Risks
25

32.2. Some suggested mitigation are:
25

33. How could the Profit Sharing Formula App be monetized?
26

34. Some costing thoughts
26

35. Pricing
27

Some considerations are:
27

36. Resources required for the Profit Sharing Formula App
27

37. Could you share your thoughts?
28

38. Price plans
28

39. Some research considerations
29

40. Return on investment
29

41. Some business plan considerations
30

42. Technical specification thoughts
30

43. How will the app be created?
31

44. Collaboration opportunities with Jack Lookman
32

45. Some suggested functionalities for the app
32

46. Demonstration Tables
33

47. Is the Profit Sharing Formula App suited to project managers?
37

48. Skills required for Profit Sharing Formula App users
37

49. Who's the project manager?
38

50. Could there be re-investments from stakeholders?
38

51. Could the project manager end up as the major stakeholder?
39

52. Exit strategy
39

53. Extra x% to the entrepreneur for historical work?
40

54. Tips on naming the app
40

55. What does the project manager bring on board?
41

56. More resources from Jack Lookman
41

57. Conclusion
42

58. Did you get value?
42

59. OTHER PUBLICATIONS BY Jack Lookman Limited 44

60. MORE RESOURCES FROM JACK LOOKMAN LIMITED 45

1. Introduction

Welcome to our series, Jack's Curated Business Ideas. This is Jack Lookman. Today's theme is: **'Profit Sharing Formula App.'**

I've done some content on the subject. This is therefore an enhancement. Please check our different platforms for more information or do a google search for Jack Lookman - Profit Sharing Formula. We hope that you enjoy the presentation and that as usual, it will stimulate other creative thoughts in you. Don't forget to articulate your thoughts; as this could come in handy, sooner or later.

The transcript of the audio presentation could be found at: jacksempowerment.com

Search for Jack's Curated Business Idea

jacksempowerment.com.   jaaloo.com.   jacklookman.co.uk

2. What's the idea?

- It's all about an app.
- One that fairly shares profit and loss with entrepreneurial or business stakeholders.
- The proposed process is more of a science than an art.
- It is fair and transparent and it quantifies inputs such as effort, money, time, etc
- And pro-rates this cumulatively when sharing profit or loss.
- It's presumably a novel idea.
- And is expected to add great value to the entrepreneurial space.

3. Inspiration for the idea

- The idea has been on my mind for a while.
- I guess that it came about during my research on getting funding and involving investors.
- Watching entrepreneurial programs like dragons den
- As well as during my entrepreneurial pursuits.
- The process of sharing profits was apparently more in favour of the investor, which is indeed for obvious reasons
- And the process appeared more like an art, than a science.
- In my opinion, there could be a better way
- As an analytical mind, I thought of doing things differently
- This is what birthed the idea.

jacksempowerment.com. jaaloo.com. jacklookman.co.uk

4. Some requirements for creating the app

- You need to have the technical specifications and brief, for the app developer.
- You need an app developer, (unless you could do it yourself).
- You need finance.
- You need to test the product.

- You need to continually upgrade and update the product.
- You need a platform for purposes of marketing and sales.
- You need to have a business plan to guide your activities.
- You need to have a monetisation plan.
- You may require a team as necessary:
    - this could be part time or full time
    - they could be permanent staff, or temporary.
    - They could actually be freelancers.
- You need to register your business
- Etc

jacksempowerment.com.   jaaloo.com.   jacklookman.co.uk

5. What are the benefits of the app?

- It's a different way of doing business collaborations.
- It's fair and transparent.
- It adds great value to concerned parties.
- It promotes accountability.
- It empowers entrepreneurs.
- It adds value to the entrepreneurial space.
- It could create opportunities.

- It could create jobs.
- It could create wealth
- It could automate processes

6. Here are some possible threats to creating a Profit Sharing Formula App.

- Trust issues
- Abuse of process
- Technical issues
- Conflict
- No due diligence
- External factors
- Abandonment
- Insufficient funds
- Business loss (no profit)
- Illness
- Death
- Under-performance of Entrepreneur
- Intellectual theft
- Copy cats
- Competition

7. Who needs the Profit Sharing Formula App?

- Entrepreneurs
- Investors
- Small scale businesses
- Collaborators

8. Opportunities for collaboration

- If you wish to collaborate on this or other projects.
- Please contact Jack Lookman via: jacklookman@yahoo.co.uk
- Use a suitable heading and short narrative.

jacksempowerment.com.   jaaloo.com.   jacklookman.co.uk

9. How does the Profit Sharing Formula App work?

- The entrepreneur does, or project manages the work.
- He shall have an agreed hourly rate.
- The same hourly rate shall apply to investors.
- This shall be modified as necessary and as mutually agreed.
- The work he does shall be timed.
- The app shall have a timer or clock.

- His time or effort shall be quantified in currency of choice and agreement e.g. £'s, $'s, etc
- If he outsources work to freelancers, he shall be paid for supervision and project management.
- Realistic budgets would have been agreed in advance
- So, will the deliverables.
- Financial inputs by investors shall be accumulated just like those of the entrepreneur's effort and investment
- At any point in time; whether monthly, quarterly, annually, etc; when it's time for profit sharing. This shall be computed by pro-rating each individual's cumulated contributions
- For example, if it's agreed to share profits every 6 months.
  - If the investors cumulative input is £3,000.00 and that of the entrepreneur is £2,000.00 total cumulative is £5,000.00.
  - If the profit to be shared is £1,000.00
  - The investor gets 3/5*1000 = £600.00
  - The entrepreneur gets £400.00

- As the collaboration journey continues
  - If the investor adds £500.00
  - And the input of the entrepreneur is £1000.00
  - And if the new profit is £2,000.00
    - the cumulative becomes £3,500.00 for the investor and £3,000.00 for the entrepreneur.
    - Total stake becomes £6,500.00

- - - By sharing £2,000.00
      - The investor gets 3.5/6.5*£2,000.00 = £1076.92
      - Entrepreneur gets 3/6.5*£2,000.00 = £923.08
      - and so on
  - The Profit Sharing Formula App computes all the figures based on inputs.
  - Please see the demonstration table later in the video.

10. Jack Lookman, have you done a video previously?

- Yes, there's some historical content on the subject.
- These are available on Youtube as well as jacksempowerment.com
- This effort is intended to add greater depth to the content.

jacksempowerment.com.   jaaloo.com.   jacklookman.co.uk

11. What's the monetisation plan?

- Product sales
- Digital adverts
- Affiliate Marketing
- Licensing
- Private label rights
- Sale of intellectual rights

12. What's the marketing plan?

- Explore different digital platforms
- Leverage different digital marketers
- Leverage your network
- Leverage traditional marketing
- Affiliate Marketing
- Social Media Marketing
- Influencer marketing
- Etc

13. Could I make passive income?

- If you get it right, it could generate passive income for a long while
- The product promises to be evergreen.
- You could also enjoy a monopoly.
- The only added required effort shall be maintenance, as necessary
- And marketing.
    - The marketing could be semi-automated

jacksempowerment.com.   jaaloo.com.   jacklookman.co.uk

14. Is it for businesses or projects?

- You could use it for either or both.
- You could also use it for multiple collaborations

15. What data needs to be inputted?

- Contact details
- Name of project or business as necessary
- Start and end time of each project management activity
- Hourly rate of project manager/ entrepreneur / investor
- Relevant narratives or notes, in brief.
- Notes with relevant 3rd parties
- Notes with investors
- Cost elements
- Targets
- Progress reports
- Profit Sharing Formula
- Monetary inflows
- Monetary outflows
- Percentage of profit to be shared
- Etc

16. What's the output data?

- Monetary inflows - total and individuals
- Monetary outflows - total and individuals
- Monetary quantification of project manager's efforts
- Profit / loss
- Cumulative monetary figures
- Profit share to each stakeholder
- Profit share to each stakeholder for x% of profit
- x could be an agreed % and could be variable
- Time spent on activities
- Money to freelancers
- Etc

jacksempowerment.com.   jaaloo.com.   jacklookman.co.uk

17. Is this effective stakeholder management?

- Yes, indeed.
- Fair, transparent, semi-automated and effective stakeholder management.

18. Who are the target audience?

- Entrepreneurs

- Project managers
- Investors
- Collaborators in all parts of the world.

19. Could collaborations be done virtually?

- Yes, they could.
- As long as you have relevant equipment, resources and the right mindset.
- Digital devices, internet connection, etc are essential.

jacksempowerment.com.   jaaloo.com.   jacklookman.co.uk

20. About Jack Lookman

- Let's pause to learn a bit about Jack Lookman.
- He's from an Engineering background
- And has varied paid and unpaid work experience.
- He's currently
    - A Content Creator
    - Multiple Author
    - Affiliate Marketer
    - Mentor
    - Entrepreneur
    - Collaborator.

21. What are the price plans for the Profit Sharing Formula App?

There could be different price plans
- Monthly payments
- Quarterly payments
- Annual payments
- Outright purchase
- It could be a license
- Etc

22. How could the app be accessed?

- It could be purchased from:
  - the iOS app store
  - Google play
  - Or suitable others.

jacksempowerment.com.   jaaloo.com.   jacklookman.co.uk

23. Could the app be synchronized?

- Yes, it could.
- With relevant other software or apps, as necessary.

24. On what gadgets could the app be used?

- Smart phones
- Digital tablets
- Laptops
- Computers

25. Is the app suitable for small or big businesses?

- The app is more suited to small businesses
    - Up and coming businesses.
    - It's more like stakeholder management on a smaller scale.

26. How could I build the app?

You could either build it yourself or outsource it to a 3rd party (app developer). You need to articulate your requirements in great detail. You could also collaborate with suitable others.

jacksempowerment.com.   jaaloo.com.   jacklookman.co.uk

27. Disclaimer

This is basically an idea. It needs to be perfected and refined. There's no guarantee of financial success. Carry out your due diligence to improve your chances of financial success.

28. Some legalities to consider

- Terms and Conditions.
- Disclaimer
- Indemnification
- Contracts between concerned parties
- General data protection regulation - for Europe.
- Intellectual rights protection.

jacksempowerment.com.   jaaloo.com.   jacklookman.co.uk

29. Possible opportunities from the Profit Sharing Formula App

- Wealth creation
- Job creation
- More entrepreneurial pursuits
- Fairer society
- Reduced crime
- Skill enhancement

30. What problem is being solved?

- Having a fairer profit share between investors and entrepreneurs.
- Having an accountable and transparent process.
- Having a more efficient sharing process.
- Process automation
- Empowerment of entrepreneurs.
- Encouragement of entrepreneurism

31. Who will fund the project?

You could explore:
- Crowdfunding
- Investors
- Bank loan
- Personal loans
- Etc

jacksempowerment.com.   jaaloo.com.   jacklookman.co.uk

32. How could risks be managed?

Under-listed are some risks and mitigations:

32.1. Risks

- Data loss
- Data compromise
- Technical issues
- Trust
- Fraud
- Litigation
- Abuse of process
- External factors

32.2. Some suggested mitigation are:

- Insurance
- Constantly updated policies and procedures
- Data back up
- Anti virus installation
- Indemnification
- Prosecution of offenders
- Terms and Conditions
- Legalities

33. How could the Profit Sharing Formula App be monetized?

- Product sales
- Mailing list
- Affiliate Marketing
- Adverts
- License
- Sale of intellectual rights
- Marketing
- Re-marketing
- Private label rights
- Etc

jacksempowerment.com. jaaloo.com. jacklookman.co.uk

34. Some costing thoughts

Some factors for consideration, are:
- Time
- Effort
- Outsourcing
- Resources used
- Freelancers
- Human resources

- Equipment used
- Rent
- Energy costs
- Etc

35. Pricing

Some considerations are:

- Costs
- Profit
- Competition
- Value
- Affordability
- Tax
- Etc

jacksempowerment.com.   jaaloo.com.   jacklookman.co.uk

36. Resources required for the Profit Sharing Formula App

- Time
- Money
- Skills

- Freelancers
- Brainstorming
- Effort
- Etc

37. Could you share your thoughts?

- What are your thoughts?
- Is it a good idea?
- What could be done better?
- What are your suggestions?
- Will you like to collaborate?
- Does the product interest you?
- Please contact Jack Lookman as necessary via jacklookman@yahoo.co.uk

38. Price plans

Payment options could be:
- Monthly
- Quarterly
- Annually
- 1-off
- Licence
- There could also be a free plan.

- This shall be packed with lots of adverts

39. Some research considerations

- Market research
- Product research
- Competitor research
- Human resource research
- Etc

jacksempowerment.com. jaaloo.com. jacklookman.co.uk

40. Return on investment

Here are some thoughts to ponder:
- What's the expected investment?
- How soon could it be recouped?
- Investments shall be in time, money, skills and effort.
- The project manager inputs time, effort and expertise and may be money.
- The investor inputs money, and time (for meetings) and may be social capital and experience.
- All inputs shall be quantified in monetary currency.
- The major resources shall be spent initially and returns could be made over the years with little major additional effort.

41. Some business plan considerations

- Name of business
- Business registration
- Business requirements
- Business model
- Financial forecast
- Budget
- Resources required
- Return on investment
- Projected break even period
- Costing
- Pricing
- Tax
- Type of product
- Competitor research
- Market research
- Product research
- Etc

jacksempowerment.com.   jaaloo.com.   jacklookman.co.uk

42. Technical specification thoughts

- Think about memory capacity

- About the job the app needs to do
- It shall be user-friendly
- Multiple computations shall be done regularly and globally.
- Choice of programming language.
- Requesting the source code, upfront.
- Requesting detailed documentation upfront.
- Synchronization with other software.
- Adaptations to different gadgets.
- Adaptations to different computer languages
- Adaptations to different platforms
- Etc

jacksempowerment.com.   jaaloo.com.   jacklookman.co.uk

43. How will the app be created?

- You could learn how to create the app via online or offline tuition
- Or outsource the creation to app developers.
- You could leverage freelancers on online platforms or suitable others.
- Tell them your requirements
    - agree on terms
    - make sure that you request the source code and detailed documentation upfront.

- These will be useful for follow up and app management.
- Get relevant training documents.
  - These could be in video, text or both
  - Request a period of grace after completion for technical support
    - usually about 1- 3 months.
    - In case of any hiccups
- take any other relevant actions.

44. Collaboration opportunities with Jack Lookman

We offer collaborative services. If interested, please contact jacklookman@yahoo.co.uk

Please use an appropriate subject heading and a short narrative

jacksempowerment.com.   jaaloo.com.   jacklookman.co.uk

45. Some suggested functionalities for the app

- It will process the inputted data
- It will present output data
- It shall have a search button
- It shall have a share button
- It shall have a timer and clock

- In addition to your time, you could input narratives of work done.
- You could include targets.
- It shall have reminders
- It shall have prompts
- It shall have a calendar
- It shall have an opt in box etc

jacksempowerment.com.   jaaloo.com.   jacklookman.co.uk

46. Demonstration Tables

Please see the demonstration below. A presumed case study. Please be informed, it contains a bit of number crunching and graphs are not included

You could also watch a detailed explanation on Youtube:

https://youtu.be/LnRZfGewWUM

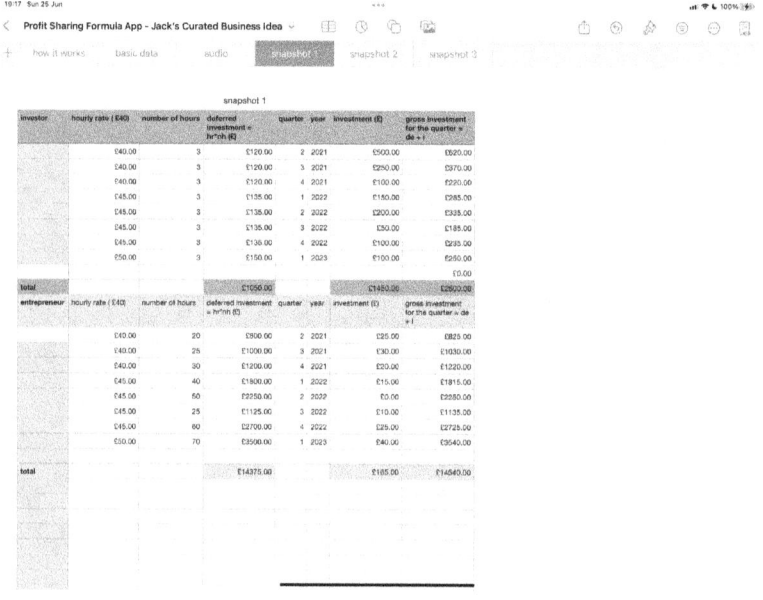

snapshot 1

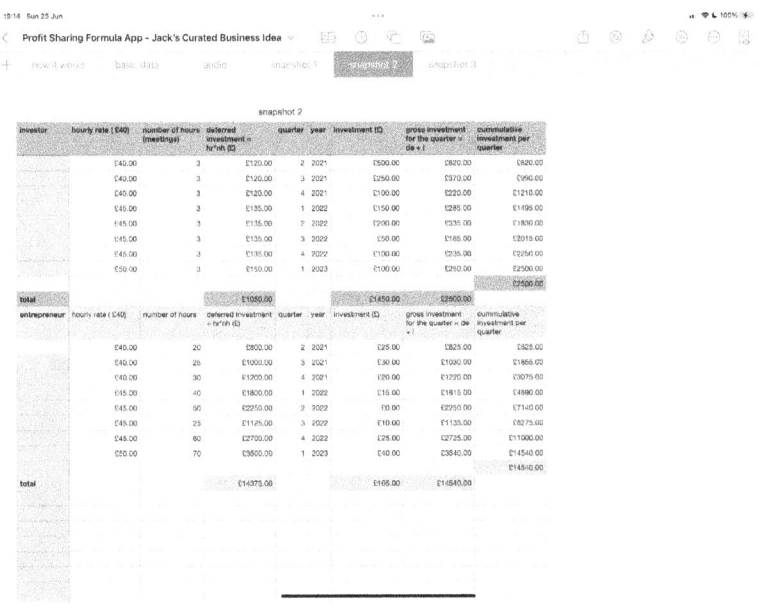

snapshot 2

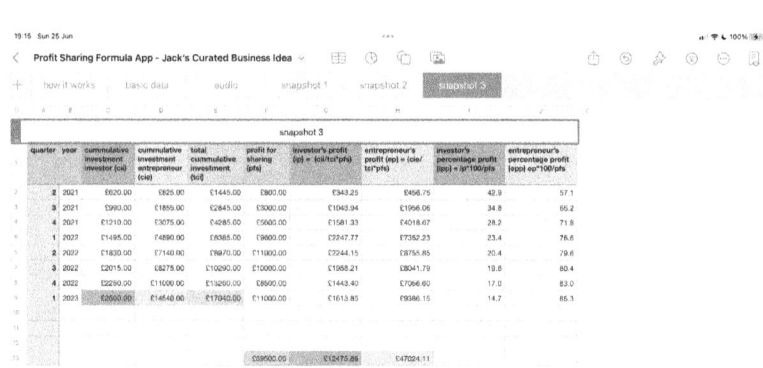

snapshot 3

47. Is the Profit Sharing Formula App suited to project managers?

- Very much so.
- The project manager shall quantify his time in supervision and solo activities.
- He shall get freelancers to bid for jobs as necessary.
- He shall oversee the work done and make payments as necessary to freelancers.

48. Skills required for Profit Sharing Formula App users

- Project management
- Costing
- Legal
- Pricing
- Interpersonal
- Numeracy
- Communication
- Negotiation
- Administrative
- Project-specific skills
- Finance
- Fundraising

- Time management
- Resource management
- Result orientation
- Budgeting
- Accounting
- Literacy
- Etc

jacksempowerment.com. jaaloo.com. jacklookman.co.uk

49. Who's the project manager?

- He's the chief executive officer or chief operations officer or entrepreneur.
- He executes the project or business while the investor finances it.
- The project manager isn't paid for his services; instead, he gets a profit share based on business success.
- He could therefore do the job as a side hustle

50. Could there be re-investments from stakeholders?

- Yes, whenever there's need for it.
- From the investors, project manager or suitable others.

jacksempowerment.com. jaaloo.com. jacklookman.co.uk

51. Could the project manager end up as the major stakeholder?

- Yes. He could end up the major shareholder even though he started as the minor financial shareholder.
- By the time his efforts accumulate, he could end up as the major stakeholder.
- He could also invest cash or recycle his dividends as necessary.
- If the project or business is successful the return on investment for all parties could be high and limitless.
- Therefore it ends up a win-win.

52. Exit strategy

- a plan shall be in place for the exit of any stakeholder
- this could be due to:
    - conflict
    - death
    - ill health
    - sale of business
    - liquidation
    - etc
- there shall be a realistic formula for parting 'gifts'

jacksempowerment.com.   jaaloo.com.   jacklookman.co.uk

53. Extra x% to the entrepreneur for historical work?

- Consider giving the Entrepreneur an extra stake
- he put in historical work and thought
- this may not be quantifiable
- this shall encourage him further
- and give him a sense of value
- this encourages him to input great value
- this is fair compromise
- the value of x shall be negotiated

Alternatively:
- quantify and approximate his historical effort
- And include this in the computations

54. Tips on naming the app

- easy name to remember
- relevant

- short

jacksempowerment.com.   jaaloo.com.   jacklookman.co.uk

55. What does the project manager bring on board?

- He brings the business idea or concept.
- He executes the business or project
- And may contribute financially.
- He also spends time, effort and expertise in project management.

56. More resources from Jack Lookman

Please check the under-listed platforms:

- jacksempowerment.com
- jacklookman.co.uk
- jaaloo.com
- Youtube - Jack Lookman
- Youtube - Business Ideas etc - Jack Lookman
- Facebook - Jack Lookman
- Facebook - Business Ideas etc - Jack Lookman
- selar.co   - Jack Lookman
- amazon.co.uk - Jack Lookman
- Internet - Jack Lookman

- Etc

jacksempowerment.com. jaaloo.com. jacklookman.co.uk

57. Conclusion

- We hope that you got value from this presentation.
- It aims to add value to the entrepreneurial space.
- It aims to make the profit sharing activity:
    - Fair
    - Efficient
    - Transparent
    - And accountable.
    - It aims to empower entrepreneurs; especially the up and coming ones.
    - It aims to marry entrepreneurship with technology.
    - The idea is apparently novel and may require perfection.

58. Did you get value?

- is this content of value?
- did you learn one or two things?
- did it stimulate other thoughts?
- could it benefit you or others?

- if yes, please check our other products and services
- some are free, and some are paid
- you may consider purchasing them
- and also gifting them to suitable others
- if you're inclined to make a donation, please send an appropriate email to jacklookman@yahoo.co.uk
- also consider liking, sharing, subscribing and reposting our Social media content

- Our mission is to Empower and Inspire Generations by leveraging the Internet

- Thank you very much for your time

jacksempowerment.com.   jaaloo.com.   jacklookman.co.uk

This is Olayinka Carew aka Jack Lookman signing off.

Ire o (I wish you blessings)

Ire kabiti (I wish you loads of blessings)

59. OTHER PUBLICATIONS BY JACK LOOKMAN LIMITED

1. Despair, Submission, Faith and Hope – Volume 1
2. Despair, Submission, Faith and Hope – Volume 2
3. Monetising Digital Book Reviews
4. E-Commerce For Traditional African Attires
5. Basic Management And Fundraising Tip For Community Groups
6. Monetising A Digital Library
7. Ajo, The App And Opportunities
8. Empowering Orphans, Widows and Widowers
9. Submission, Gratitude, Faith and Hope
10. Oro Ishiti- Indelible Yoruba Words
11. Eid Monetisation by Leveraging Technology
12. What are your thoughts? What is your mindset? - Volume 1
13. What are your thoughts? What is your mindset? - Volume 2
14. Twenty Curated Business Ideas - Volume 1
15. Jaaloo Puzzles - Volume 1
16. Jaaloo Puzzles - Volume 2
17. Beauty Of The Storm
18. Digital Career Guidance App
19. Bath Sponge Project
20. Monetising Jollof Rice
21. Leasing Digital Tablets / Gadgets To Undergraduates

22. Event Discount App

60. MORE RESOURCES FROM JACK LOOKMAN LIMITED

Olayinka Carew aka Jack Lookman

Jaaloo: https://www.jaaloo.com

Jack's Empowerment: https://www.jacksempowerment.com

Jack Lookman: https://jacklookman.co.uk

Amazon books: https://amzn.to/3jahxEC   (or search for Jack Lookman at amazon.com)

Become a member of Jack Lookman's Facebook Community: https://www.facebook.com/jack.lookman.3

As well as at : Opo Ati Orukan: https://bit.ly/OpoAtiOrukan

Facebook group: Business Ideas etc: https://bit.ly/BusinessIdeasetc

Oro Ishiti- Indelible Yoruba Words - Youtube channel - https://bit.ly/oroishitiytc

Subscribe to Jack Lookman's Youtube Channel: https://bit.ly/JackLookman (or search for Jack Lookman)

Business Ideas etc (Youtube channel): https://youtube.com/@businessideasetc5620

Ebooks on Selar:

https://selar.co/m/jacklookman?affiliate=ercg

Books - Amazon - https://www.amazon.co.uk/s?k=jack+lookman&crid=Y127BR5D0SS3&sprefix=,aps,50&ref=nb_s_b_ss_recent_1_0_recent

Jack's Mentoring 101: https://www.jacksempowerment.com/products/courses/view/1152633

Connect on LinkedIn: Olayinka Carew aka Jack Lookman

Or Jack Lookman on Facebook messenger

Email: jacklookman@yahoo.co.uk

At Jack Lookman Limited there are opportunities for mentees, investors, donors and collaborators.

jacksempowerment.com.   jacklookman.co.uk.   jaaloo.com

#jackscuratedbusinessideas

#ProfitSharingFormulaApp

#ProfitSharingFormula

#JackLookman

#jackscuratedbusinessidea

#EmpowermentandInspiration

#empoweringandinspiringgenerations

#OurmissionistoEmpowerandInspireGenerationsbyleveragingtheInternet

#ireo

#Irekabiti

#JackLookman

#mrjaaloo

www.ingramcontent.com/pod-product-compliance
Lightning Source LLC
Chambersburg PA
CBHW030038230526
45472CB00002B/561